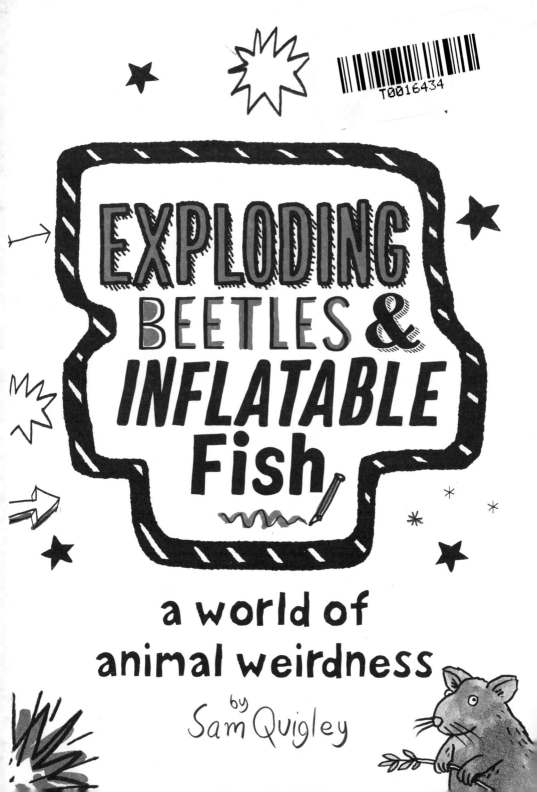

EXPLODING BEETLES & INFLATABLE Fish

a world of animal weirdness

by Sam Quigley

A Raspberry Book
Text: Tracey Turner
Art: Andrew Wightman
Cover design: Sidonie Beresford-Browne
Art direction: Sidonie Beresford-Browne
Internal design: Amy McHugh

KINGFISHER
LONDON & NEW YORK

First published 2021 in the United States by Kingfisher
This edition published 2023 in the United States by Kingfisher
120 Broadway, New York, NY 10271
Kingfisher is an imprint of Macmillan Children's Books, London
All rights reserved

ISBN 978-0-7534-7625-3 (HB)
978-0-7534-7641-3 (PB)

Library of Congress Cataloging-in-Publication data has been applied for.

Kingfisher books are available for special promotions and premiums.
For details contact:
Special Markets Department, Macmillan,
120 Broadway, New York, NY 10271

For more information please visit:
www.kingfisherbooks.com

Printed in China
1 3 5 7 9 8 6 4 2
1TR/0123/RV/WKT/115WF

MIX
Paper | Supporting
responsible forestry
FSC® C116313

EXPLODING BEETLES & INFLATABLE Fish

a world of animal weirdness

KINGFISHER
LONDON & NEW YORK

A FEW THINGS ABOUT ME:

My name's **Sam Quigley**. This can be annoying because sometimes unbelievably immature people call me names like **Squiggly**, **Wiggly**, or **Jiggly**. But it could be a lot worse. For example, there is someone in my class named Brad Shufflebottom.

※ I have pets. They are:

Two stick insects named

Twiggy

and

Wiggy

A hamster named **Letty** ⟹

A goldfish named **Bob**

✳ I really like interesting facts. Things like **the tallest building in the world is the Burj Khalifa in Dubai and it's 2,717 feet (828 meters) tall** are quite interesting, but what I really like are things like

there's a type of lizard that can walk on water

the Fourth Duke of Northumberland invented a wasp gun—like, for killing wasps

flamingos keep <u>cool</u> by peeing down their legs

✳ I have a sister and brother who are quite a bit older than me. They can be annoying and sometimes try to stop me from keeping toads in the bath and things like that. But they're all right really.

Am I as interesting as a stick insect?

Here are a few facts about stick insects, and **personally** I think they're quite a bit more interesting than most people I know.

Twiggy and Wiggy

are Indian stick insects.

Their favorite food is leaves from a **blackberry bush**. I keep them in a glass tank called a vivarium (actually a neighbor's old fish tank but **vivarium** sounds much better).

Some Interesting Things About **Stick Insects**:

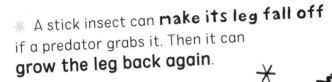

✳ A stick insect can **make its leg fall off** if a predator grabs it. Then it can **grow the leg back again**.

✳ There are more than 3,000 different types of stick insect, and not all of them look like **sticks**—some look like **leaves**.

✳ Stick insects look like sticks (or leaves) so they can hide from **animals that want to eat them** (obviously). Some can even **change color** to blend in with their surroundings, like **chameleons** do.

✳ Stick insects shed their skin and grow a new one. **They often eat the old skin.**

✳ Some kinds of stick insect **sway from side to side**, which looks really weird.

✳ To defend themselves, some stick insects make a **foul-smelling liquid ooze from their joints**, and some of them spray a **nasty chemical** at attackers.

which reminds me of something . . .

Have you ever heard of **bombardier beetles**?
They are some of the coolest insects in the world because
—and I am honestly not joking—they fire **poisonous
chemicals from their butts** at attackers. They are like
living toxic water pistols.

HERE'S HOW
IT WORKS:

**EXPLOSIVE
GAS 100%**

There are **two different
chemicals** in separate
parts of the beetle's body.
When it's threatened by
a predator, the beetle can
mix the chemicals together.
The chemicals react and
reach the boiling point. Then
the beetle takes aim with
its butt and fires the hot,
toxic spray at the attacker.

**EXPLOSION
CHAMBER**

Ready, aim, **FIRE** ...
it even makes a
POP! sound.

It's enough to kill some kinds of predator.

If a bombardier beetle does get eaten by, say, a toad, it can **survive in the toad's stomach** for up to two hours. Sometimes the toad is irritated by the beetle's chemicals inside its stomach and is **sick**, and the beetle comes out alive and well, **ready to explode another day.**

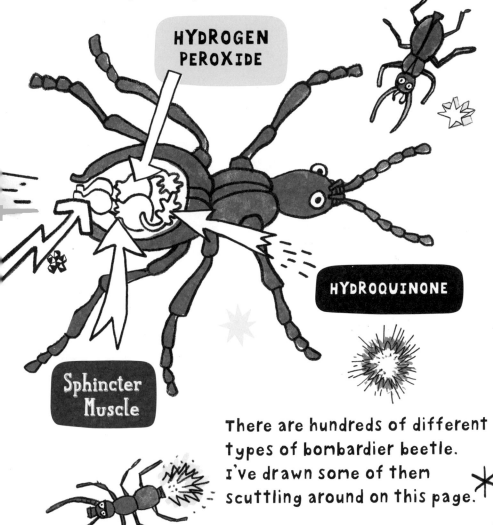

HYDROGEN PEROXIDE

HYDROQUINONE

Sphincter Muscle

There are hundreds of different types of bombardier beetle. I've drawn some of them scuttling around on this page.

I am QUITE GLAD Twiggy and Wiggy can't explode.

I make sure they always have lots of leaves to eat. To keep them fresh I cut branches from a blackberry bush or a hedge and put them in a container half-full of water inside the vivarium. Stick insects don't like wilted leaves, and **who can blame them?**

All that eating can only mean **one thing:**

a lot of POOPING!

And because stick insects need to be kept quite warm, **mold can start to grow on the poop.**

That would be GROSS, so once a week it's **cleaning time**—I decided to do it when I got home from school today.

This is what I do . . .

1. I take Twiggy and Wiggy out and **they crawl up my arms** for a bit.

2. I put them in a box with holes in the lid.

3. I take everything out of the vivarium and change the newspaper at the bottom of it.

4. I clean the glass with a bit of paper towel.

5. I put in clean newspaper (or sometimes paper towel).

6. I put everything back into the vivarium again. **Not forgetting** Twiggy and Wiggy.

Twiggy and Wiggy look **really** pleased.

Actually, they look exactly the same as they always do.

IT'S EASY. One is about half an inch (1.2 cm) bigger than the other one. Wiggy is about 2 3/4 inches (7 cm) long and Twiggy is 3 1/4 inches (8 cm). **PLUS** Twiggy supports the Patriots while Wiggy is a Colts fan. (Not really! They are BOTH Patriots supporters, **obviously**.)

But 3 1/4 inches is **NOTHING** compared to the world's longest stick insect, which is an insect of **EPIC proportions**.

It was bred at the Insect Museum of Western China, and it was 25 inches (64 cm) long.

That's **even longer** than my mom's arm.

It is the **longest**

insect in the world...

...as well as the longest stick insect.

My brother Joe doesn't like insects much—at least, not as much as I do. *(Then again, I guess that is most people.)* He thinks **I'm** a bit weird for keeping them as pets in my bedroom. But I don't think pets **have** to be furry.

And Twiggy and Wiggy **ARE CUTE** no matter what he says.

There are some insects that are **REALLY WEIRD**, mind you...

Just take a look at these.
I give you . . .

THE BRAZILIAN
TREEHOPPER.

It is not wearing a hat. Haha.

These **aren't** eyes. No one knows what the crazy ball things are for —they might be telling predators to go away.

This looks a bit like a thorn, **maybe camouflage**?

Bristles— **who knows?**— might help the insect sense the world around it.

They live in trees in the
BRAZILIAN RAIN FOREST
and eat sap from leaves.

They only grow to about $\frac{1}{4}$ **inch (6 mm) long.**

There are **1000s** of kinds of treehopper but not all of them look **weird**.

And . . .

THE GIRAFFE WEEVIL

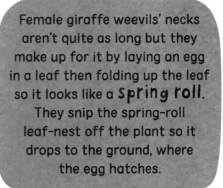

Males use their long necks **to fight each other**.

Female giraffe weevils' necks aren't quite as long but they make up for it by laying an egg in a leaf then folding up the leaf so it looks like a **spring roll**. They snip the spring-roll leaf-nest off the plant so it drops to the ground, where the egg hatches.

Giraffe weevils live only on the island of Madagascar in the Indian Ocean. All sorts of unique animals live there.

The wing cases are bright red.

※ When writers and film makers and artists are looking for inspiration for alien beings, they sometimes look at the insect world. Which is no surprise. These two would make **really good aliens**.

Anyway, enough about weird insects because my Bob's Feeding Time alarm has just gone off.

I always feed Bob at the same time of day and give him **one pinch of fish food**. It's really important to remember whether or not I've fed him because **goldfish don't have stomachs**, so they don't know when they're full. So, if you feed them too much they **just keep eating** until they get sick.

pop!

Some Reasons Goldfish ARE Interesting

(And NOT AT ALL Boring Like My Brother Says)

I feed Bob fish food that I buy from the pet shop, but **goldfish will eat lots of things**, like plants, smaller creatures (like tadpoles), AND THEIR OWN POOP. Sorry, but it's true.

pop!

Goldfish do **NOT** have a 3-second memory.

They can identify **shapes, colors, and sounds,** and they can be taught to do **tricks** like pushing a ball through a hoop (Bob does this!).

You know how you can tell the age of a tree by counting the number of rings inside the trunk? Goldfish are a bit like that too. They have **tiny rings on their scales** that you can only see using a microscope. **You can tell their age by the number of rings**—one for every year they live.

Most goldfish are quite small, but that's usually because of the size of the tank they're kept in. **(Don't keep them in a bowl!)** They need lots of room to be happy.

Bob will eat his fish food from my finger but there are some fish you definitely would not want to feed by hand . . .

PIRANHAS!

Their teeth are triangular and as sharp as razors. But there are people who keep piranhas as pets.

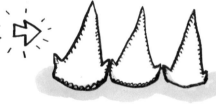

(WHY?? Don't they want their fingers?)

There are about 60 different kinds of piranha.

This is a **red-bellied piranha.**

It's the biggest kind with the sharpest teeth and most powerful jaws.

They hunt in groups of up to 100.

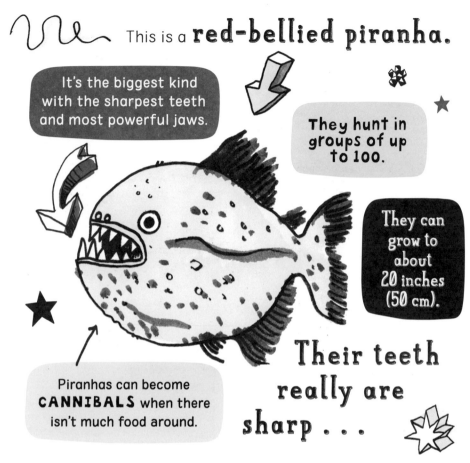

They can grow to about 20 inches (50 cm).

Piranhas can become **CANNIBALS** when there isn't much food around.

Their teeth really are sharp . . .

✳ Piranhas do sometimes **bite people's fingers and toes off** in rivers in South America (where piranhas live), but they usually attack animals that aren't much bigger than they are.

✳ People say that if you walked into a river where there are piranhas, **you would be a skeleton in five minutes—** but that would **NOT** really happen.

There are meat-eating fish that live in the sea that also have a **bad reputation** . . .

SHARKS!

You'd think sharks attack people all the time,

but they don't.

I'm not saying you
should jump into the
sea when there are
big sharks around and
it's shark dinner time (often dawn and dusk,
if you're interested, but you never really know).

I just think everyone should calm down a bit . . .

Great white sharks, tiger sharks, and bull sharks have
all been known to kill people (and a few other kinds of
sharks as well) but there are about **400 kinds of shark**
and most are **completely harmless**.

Around five people get killed by sharks every year. **BUT** think about this:

* Road traffic accidents kill more than a million people per year.

People kill 100 million sharks and rays every year.

So, it's a bit **IRONIC** for **US** to talk about **SHARKS** being dangerous.

By the way, **the animal that kills most people** in the world hasn't got massive teeth and isn't obviously scary like a tiger or a snake.

It's the small but deadly
malarial mosquito.

It's tiny, but it kills hundreds of thousands of people every year by spreading a **horrible disease** called malaria.

Bob just looks like a fish, but there are some **really funny-looking goldfish**.

There are some kinds with BIG BUG EYES or long frilly fins and tails, but the funniest-looking one of the lot is the **bubble eye goldfish.**

Its eyes point upward.

It has a huge balloon-like sac on each side of its head.

A deep-sea fish called the **blobfish** was voted the

WORLD'S UGLIEST FISH

by the Ugly Animals Preservation Society.
Here's why:

For a bit of extra weirdness,
blobfish sit on their eggs until
they hatch, just like birds do.

I don't think the blobfish is the
World's Most Disgusting Animal, though...

... I think that prize should go to

The slimiest animal in the world (probably) is the hagfish. I think it's also the world's most disgusting creature, but you decide.

It . . .

. . . has rows of sharp teeth on its tongue.

. . . can digest its food through its skin.

. . . slithers inside rotting carcasses in the ocean and eats them (hagfish are the vultures of the sea).

The HORRIBLE HAGFISH!

... produces an amazing amount of slime if it feels threatened.

... is extremely ugly (sorry, hagfish).

If you put a hagfish in a bucket of water, the whole bucket would turn to the most **revolting slime** in a matter of seconds.

Eewwww!

I made myself feel a **bit sick** thinking about hagfish, so I gave the plants in my bedroom some water instead.

I have some **CACTUSES** that hardly ever need watering. They like it on the windowsill where they get lots of sun.

My ferns like a bit more shade and need watering every few days. One's got a few dead parts on it that I'll have to cut off.

I have one plant that is unusual and, to be honest, a bit disgusting *(nowhere near as disgusting as the hagfish though—yuck!).*

It's a **carnivorous pitcher plant**.

There are lots of different kinds. This one needs lots of light like my cactuses, but it also needs lots of water.

There's nectar inside these weird parts. Insects come looking for the nectar.

The insects get trapped and die and the plant digests them!

I'd forgotten to do something for Twiggy and Wiggy. I'm **supposed** to spray the inside of their vivarium with water every couple of days. So I got the plant-mister and opened the vivarium—**and that's when I realized.**

Something terrible has happened.

There was only ONE stick insect inside.

I double-checked, triple-checked, and quadruple-checked (because stick insects are very good at hiding). *But there is definitely only one stick insect in there.*

Twiggy has gone <u>missing.</u>

I've looked **everywhere** in my bedroom. I turned out **all** the drawers.

We had spaghetti Bolognese for dinner but I couldn't eat much of it. Joe looked at me picking at my food and said:

> **Let me guess. One of your animals has escaped.**

Which was really unhelpful.

Mom said:

Don't worry Sam. I'm sure Twiggy will turn up.

But I've already searched my bedroom. If Twiggy isn't there, **where else could she be?** Maybe she won't turn up.

Mom said there was ice cream. But **even salted caramel flavor can't make me feel any better**.

I've now checked:

- ☑ **My bedroom**
- ☑ **The living room**
- ☑ **The bathroom**

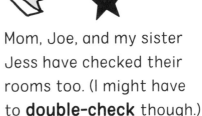

Mom, Joe, and my sister Jess have checked their rooms too. (I might have to **double-check** though.)

NO TWIGGY.

There's a **no-vacuuming** rule until Twiggy is found.

A terrible thought occurred to me. **Could the pitcher plant have eaten Twiggy?**

There was only one way to find out.
The last time I saw Twiggy was only a couple of hours ago. If she'd somehow managed to crawl up into the pitcher plant and fall in . . . she'd still be there.

So I summoned up all my courage and had a look in the pitchers.

NO TWIGGY

THANK YOU UNIVERSE!

There were some tiny little flies in some of the pitchers, which was horrible enough.

Twiggy probably wouldn't be interested in the pitcher plant anyway, because she eats leaves and not nectar.

Also, I think she would be too big for it.

※ The **biggest carnivorous plant in the world is a type of pitcher plant**—the pitchers can hold nearly a gallon (4 liters) so Twiggy wouldn't be too big for that.

※ It can eat animals even bigger than Letty!

(Ugh).

I was looking for Twiggy in the hallway
when my Letty's Feeding Time alarm went off.

Letty's cage is on a shelf in the hallway, where it's usually
quite quiet during the day. We only turn on a dim
light in the hall in the evenings because . . .

Hamsters are nocturnal

. . . which is why I don't keep
Letty in my bedroom.

TODAY'S MENU IS:

Pet shop hamster food

Side order of chopped carrot and apple
(actually the remains of my lunchbox)

Pumpkin seed garnish

Drinks:
tap water
(freshly
changed
dispenser)

Treats:
Once a week
or so, Letty
gets a bit of
hard-boiled
egg as a
special treat.

I was just wondering what she'd be eating if she was in the wild (she's a Syrian hamster).

HERE'S WHAT I FOUND OUT:

SEEDS
e.g. sunflower seeds

CEREALS
e.g. wheat

INSECT LARVAE
e.g. caterpillars

INSECTS
e.g. crickets

Wait.

Insects

e.g. crickets?

Surely Letty wouldn't eat Twiggy?

Twiggy would have to squeeze herself into Letty's cage through the bars. So it's probably impossible.

RIGHT. Stick insects are good at hiding. What are they hiding from?

What eats stick insects?

Here's what I found out . . .

EVERYTHING!

Birds, reptiles, rodents, spiders . . . even other insects, if they're big enough.

That's why stick insects are so good at looking **STICKY**. And all the other things like oozing horrible liquid from their joints and spraying chemicals (not as good as the bombardier beetle, but still). I also just found out that some kinds of stick insect **VOMIT** foul-tasting liquid if something tries to eat them, to see if that puts it off.

Jess said instead of looking in dark places like under the sink and in Mom's sock drawer, we should be looking around us to see if Twiggy is blending in with anything that looks a bit like a stick.

Because she is probably . . .

HIDING IN PLAIN SIGHT.

It's dark outside now, but tomorrow (which helpfully is Saturday) I will start looking for sticks.

I've been up since 6 am searching the yard.
The yard isn't very big but obviously there are a lot of twigs and sticks in it, i.e. places to hide if you're a stick insect.

There is STILL no Twiggy.

I found about **a hundred** other things though.

✳ **LOTS of beetles**—this is not surprising because there are more types of beetle in the world than any other type of animal. ⟶

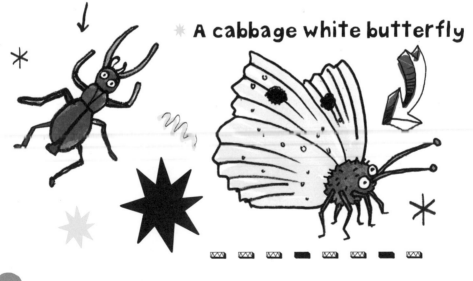

✳ **A cabbage white butterfly**

woodlice, which aren't beetles by the way. They're crustaceans, and relatives of crabs and lobsters. **They have 14 legs and breathe through gills,** because their ancestors used to live in water millions of years ago. They like dark places and they eat . . .

Rotten wood and plants
Mushrooms *and other fungi*
Woodlouse poop

Yes, woodlice eat their own poop, but you'll be glad to know they don't also drink their own pee.

In fact, **woodlice don't pee at all**. Instead they make a chemical called ammonia, which smells really strong and comes wafting out of their shells as a gas.

Imagine if people did that.

No, actually, don't.

It's very twiggy underneath the green leaves and flowers of the honeysuckle plant, so I took a really close look. **But there was no stick insect.**

There were **a lot of ants** though, especially after Jess came out to help me look and dropped her apple on the path.

Ants are amazing animals.

There are more than 12,000 different kinds (one has a lifespan of 30 years)!

They're social animals and send signals to one another by leaving a chemical scent trail.

They can lift **50 times their own weight** and sometimes work together to lift even bigger things.

You'd hardly notice if one of the ants in my yard bit you on the leg, but there's a type of ant that is supposed to have the **most painful sting of any insect in the world** . . .

Being stung by a **bullet ant** feels like **being shot with a bullet** (which is why they got their name).

The pain makes people **throw up or pass out**, and you're in agony for around 24 hours.

Some people in the Amazon rain forest, where the ant comes from, have a special ceremony for teenage boys that involves being stung **HUNDREDS OF TIMES** by bullet ants to show that they are **AS HARD AS NAILS**.

And, to be fair, they totally must be.

Joe came into the yard to help look for Twiggy as well, but he was only here for about five minutes before he screamed and did a dance and went rushing back inside.

He <u>hates</u> spiders

and one had crawled down his T-shirt.

I know people have **IRRATIONAL FEARS** but how many people are terrified of, say,

SQUIRRELS?

I bet a squirrel, with its big sharp teeth, could do you a lot more damage than a **tiny spider**.

Did you know the thread spiders spin to make their webs is stronger than steel? Yes, the stuff that comes completely naturally out of something that **looks very much like a butt** is stronger than a metal made by people using a blast furnace.

There are a few spiders that can hurt people. One of the most dangerous is the

Brazilian wandering spider.

It is **FIERCE** (if you saw one and gave it a poke it would definitely want to fight you).

It can **JUMP!**

It sometimes travels the world in bunches of bananas . . .

It has a bite that can **KILL PEOPLE.**

. . . so watch out!

A BRAZILIAN WANDERING SPIDER WOULD DEFINITELY EAT A STICK INSECT.

Would one of the spiders in the yard?

Maybe, if it was a really big one . . .

We have a little pond in our yard because they **encourage biodiversity** according to Jess. It's an old-fashioned tin bath that Mom recycled by burying most of it in the soil and putting some plants and things in it.

Which reminded me that there are spiders that can walk on water—**fishing spiders**. Their legs are covered with waterproof hairs, and that's how they float. They can bounce along the surface of the water, flying into the air then bouncing off the water again.

BOING BOING BOING BOING

There are more than a thousand different types of animal that can **walk on water** and there are some in our pond—little insects called **water boatmen** and WATER STRIDERS.

Pygmy geckos are **tiny lizards** that live in the Amazon rain forest. They are so small and light that they can walk on the water's surface too.

Basilisk lizards are much heavier, but they can run across water on their hind legs for about 15 feet (4.5 m) —they have to keep running, though, otherwise they sink.

As far as I know, stick insects **CAN'T** walk on water. So the pond is yet another potential Twiggy . . .

...DEATH TRAP.

There was **no sign** of Twiggy in the plants by the pond.

There were lots of other things, though, including a **dragonfly**.

Dragonflies lay their eggs in water.

Then the eggs hatch into things that look like **absolute monsters**.

They are completely ferocious.

Anything small enough for them to eat doesn't stand a chance.

There was also quite a lot of **green gloopy stuff** called **blanket weed** in the pond.

We have to get rid of blanket weed by winding it around a stick—otherwise it **completely takes over**. You have to take it out and leave it on the side of the pond for a day, so any creatures in the weed can get back into the pond. Then you can put the weed in the compost bin.

IT'S REALLY GLOOPY AND HORRIBLE.

Talking of **gloopy** and **horrible**, there are other disgusting deep-sea animals that give the hagfish a bit of competition.

LIKE . . .

The BLACK SWALLOWER.

It has a hideous, huge stretchy stomach so it can swallow prey **TWICE AS BIG AS ITSELF**.

It can live more than 1.6 miles (2.5 km) deep.

It eats mostly fish.

GULP.

✳ A black swallower can swallow a fish so big it starts to rot inside the massive stomach before it's digested. As it rots, the dead fish **makes so much gas** that it pushes the black swallower up to the top of the sea.

Blecchhh!!

✳ A black swallower was found with a fish in its stomach that measured **34 inches (86 cm) long**—more than four times as long as the black swallower itself.

DOUBLE BLECH!!

And there are lots more.

Unlike the black swallower, which **LURKS UNSEEN**, lots of deep-sea creatures glow in the dark. one is the

COOKIE-CUTTER SHARK.

It has a green glow and gets its name because it **BITES ROUND HOLES** out of other creatures while they're still alive (ugh). The animals don't die—the hole eventually heals up leaving a scar in the shape of a circle.

Cookie cutters sometimes leave bite marks on submarines and undersea cables as well.

Some of the fish that live really deep in the sea have lights to attract other fish. As soon as the unsuspecting fish get close enough . . .

CHOMP!

* The **dragonfish** has a light hanging from its lower jaw.

* The **anglerfish** dangles a glowing light just above its toothy mouth.

* The **VIPERFISH** has a light that hangs just above its mouth (filled with lots of needle-y teeth) AND see-through skin—just to be extra horrible.

Unlike our pond, there's bone-crushing pressure where these weird little fish live. You'd be squished **instantly** if you weren't inside a submarine.

I'd just finished fishing out the last of the slimy green weed when a toad **jumped** out of the pond.

It hopped off into the undergrowth.

I built a frog and toad house out of broken plant pots a while ago so they have somewhere nice and damp to live when they're not in the pond. I reckon the toad was off to hang out in it.

OBVIOUSLY a toad would eat a stick insect, because, as I found out, just about **everything** would eat a stick insect.

A frog would also eat a stick insect **(see above)**.

By the way, do you know the difference between frogs and toads?

Which is the **frog** and which is the **toad**?

VS.

* Toads have thicker, bumpier, drier skin, while a frog's skin is smooth and slimy.

* Frogs have **longer, more powerful hind legs** than toads (so toads mostly walk instead of hopping).

* **Toads lay their eggs in long strings or chains**—frogs lay them in a clump.

* There are exceptions, though, and sometimes toads are commonly known as frogs, e.g. the **harlequin frog** (which is a toad).

* By the way, **it's not true about toads giving you warts**. Feel free to stroke a toad any time you like.

As long as the toad doesn't mind.

Do you know what the

MOST POISONOUS THING in the world is?

Take a guess. Is it a . . .

Snake
Jellyfish
Spider
Scorpion
Beetle
Frog?

You might be surprised about the answer to this.

Or maybe not, since I've just been talking about frogs and toads. It's a

FROG.

The most poisonous creature on Earth is the

golden poison frog.

They live in the colombian rain forest.

They're only about 2 inches (5 cm long).

Each one contains about a milligram of poison on its skin.

That's **enough to kill ten people!**

✳ The Emberá people in Colombia use the frog's poison on the tips of their blowgun darts when they go hunting.

✳ The golden poison frog is **poisonous**—which means it doesn't inject venom. That reminds me of something . . .

Some people eat poisonous creatures on purpose, which seems like a **completely crazy** thing to do.

PUFFERFISH

look pretty ordinary when they're just swimming along, but when they're **threatened by a predator** they do this:

Pufferfish gulp lots of water to make them **blow up.**

It's an **INFLATABLE FISH!**

Some kinds of pufferfish have spines so they're even more difficult to eat. It makes it **almost impossible** for a predator to eat them.

✳ There are around **120 different types of pufferfish**— the biggest one measures about 24 inches (60 cm) long.

✳ If a predator does eat a pufferfish, it will have a **very bad taste** in its mouth and might die because pufferfish are **poisonous**.

Pufferfish poison is DEADLY to people.

✳ Pufferfish are an expensive treat in Japan, where they're known as **fugu**.

✳ If you want to eat a pufferfish in a restaurant **(WHY??)**, you will need a lot of money because it's very expensive.

✳ Chefs have to train for years before they're allowed to prepare and cook a pufferfish, **so that it doesn't poison people.**

The neighbor's cat, **Pascoe**, jumped into the yard and started purring and rubbing his head against my legs. **He's a really nice cat.**

BUT WOULD HE EAT A STICK INSECT?

❋ I've seen him sitting by next door's garden pond—which has **goldfish** in it—staying very still and **staring into the water.**

❋ I'm pretty sure that if he had the chance he would **eat** one of the fish.

❋ **I don't think he ever has though.**

I have never seen him stalking
a spider or a big insect.
But I wouldn't put it past him—
cats are hunters.

SOME INTERESTING
CAT FACTS:

✳ In Ancient Egypt cats **were sacred.**
When a pet cat died, the owners
shaved off their eyebrows
to show how sad they were.

✳ A **male** cat is called a **tom** and
a **female** cat is called a **queen.**

✳ Kittens meow to one another, but
adult cats don't meow to communicate
with other cats—they meow to
communicate with people!

I've now covered every last inch of the yard.

I know stick insects are good at **camouflage,** but I've been looking really carefully and **I CAN'T BELIEVE I'VE MISSED TWIGGY—** if she was here, I'd have found her.

There are lots of animals that are good at hiding like Twiggy. **Seahorses** can look just like coral . . .

. . . and some **caterpillars** look like moss.

There are **geckos** that are almost invisible when they're on a tree trunk. There are also **moths**, **frogs**, and **owls** that are really hard to see against tree bark.

Some geckos look like dead leaves.

There are **praying mantises** that look like twigs, moss, dead leaves, and even orchids. They're CAMOUFLAGED to hide from their prey, not from predators. They lie in wait and then...

...POUNCE!

Mom came outside to hang up some washing.
She made sure to check where she was walking,
in case she stepped on a small animal (she is very
good at this now), and **narrowly missed a snail.**

Mom loves her garden plants and **snails and slugs**
sometimes eat them, but she'd never use
slug pellets—they kill slugs and snails
but they also kill the birds and other
things that eat them.

Animals like . . .

OPOSSUMS

I ask you, who could possibly want to hurt an opossum? I mean, fair enough, they are completely covered in fleas. But **look at their little faces.**

NO LUCK FINDING TWIGGY, SAM?

Mom asked—even though it was pretty obvious that

I HADN'T FOUND TWIGGY.

Mom said: Have I ever told you the story of Mr. Barker?

I said: NO?

Even though I've heard it **loads** of times before. So she told me the story again.

Mr. Barker was Mom's dog when she was a child (back in the days BEFORE THE INTERNET).

One day they moved to a different town and Mr. Barker was **accidentally left behind.**

I think Grandad thought the dog was traveling in Grandma's car **(or probably horse and cart in those days)**, and Grandma thought Mr. Barker was in Grandad's car, or something.

Anyway, he got left behind and when they realized, they rushed back to pick him up. **But he wasn't there.** The people who moved into the old house hadn't seen him.

The whole family **loved** Mr. Barker—he was a cute scruffy dog like my friend Alex's dog—and they were all **VERY** sad. They stuck posters up all over the place in their old town and asked all their friends and neighbors about him. Dogs and cats didn't have microchips in those days **(what with it being the Cretaceous Period).**

But one day, **A WHOLE MONTH** after they'd moved, they heard something **scraping** at their back door. It was . . .

A BURGLAR.

NOT REALLY.

It was Mr. Barker!

All skinny and dirty and covered with fleas. He had **RETURNED!** They never found out how he'd managed to find them.

They had a massive party to celebrate —once they'd gotten rid of Mr. Barker's fleas and given him a bath.

He lived happily ever after.

There are lots of stories about dogs and cats who get lost and find their way home. Some are **missing for MONTHS and travel hundreds of miles** and then turn up at their owner's house looking even worse than Mr. Barker did.

But Twiggy is not a dog or a cat. She is a stick insect, which are not famous for their loyalty. On the other hand, they ARE famous for being the prey of lots of other animals.

AND THERE IS STILL NO SIGN OF HER.

I find myself looking suspiciously at **every animal** I see as a potential
TWIGGY MURDERER.

By the time it was bedtime I **went to sleep** thinking of
ALL THE NOCTURNAL ANIMALS that
might be **lying in wait to ambush** a stick insect.
Things like **moths** (it would need to be quite a big moth).
And ...

BATS

Sometimes we see bats flying around near our house at night.

✴ They swoop around eating **flying** insects, but they would **definitely** eat a **stick insect** if they saw one.

❋ **Bats look a bit like mice**—some do, anyway (and quite a few have ugly little scrunched-up faces). But they're more closely related to monkeys, which I thought was **quite surprising.**

❋ By the way, bats aren't blind—they can see, but most bats' eyesight isn't all that good, so they find their way around using . . .

...echolocation.

❋ **They make squeaky noises** and figure out where things are by the way the sound bounces back to them. **Which is really clever.**

❋ Not all bats use echolocation—**fruit bats** have **enormous** eyes and can see really well, so they don't need it.

❋ The **biggest** bat in the world is a **fruit bat,** and its wingspan can be **6 feet (1.8 m) wide!**

VAMPIRE BATS

come out at night and use echolocation to find their way around, but **they're not after insects.**

They're after . . .

BLOOD!

- Specifically, the blood of big animals like horses or cows, or maybe even people. Once they've found an animal, they make a **little cut with their sharp pointy fangs,** and then lap up the blood. Their spit contains a painkiller so the horse doesn't feel anything, and a blood thinner to keep the **blood flowing.**

* Vampire bats don't kill the animals they feed on, but the cuts might become infected.

* Sometimes vampire bats carry the deadly disease rabies, which makes you **FOAM AT THE MOUTH** and go mad (and then die).

Vampire bats

are the only mammals that live on blood alone.

At least they wouldn't be interested in

TWIGGY.

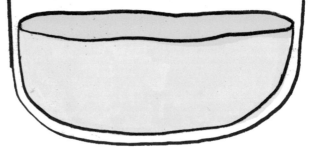

I left some **leafy twigs** in a jar of water on my windowsill for Twiggy, **just in case they lure her back**.

It's sort of unlikely, though, as blackberry bushes are very common plants so it's not as if Twiggy would be short of something to eat if I wasn't feeding her.

My friends **Lily and Alex** came over to help me look. They both have pets, so they understand.

LILY HAS A CAT THAT IS COMPLETELY EVIL.

He's named Washington (I am not sure why he is named after a president, and **no one can give me a good answer**), he is very old, and he waits for people to walk past him so that he can . . .

...swipe at them viciously.

✳ Lily is the only person Washington likes. He sits on her lap and lets Lily **tickle his tummy**. If anyone else tried to do that, I dread to think what that cat would do. I would **NEVER** try it.

✳ Lily says Washington has always been like this and no one knows why.

✳ Apart from Lily, I'm not sure how hard anyone would look if Washington went missing.

ALEX HAS LOTS OF PETS.

There is **Mungo**, a Scottie dog with a hatred of squirrels, Tallulah, a big, scruffy dog who likes cheese, being stroked, and leaning against people, and some reptiles . . .

A tortoise named George.

* No one is quite sure how old George is because he was given to Alex's mom by her uncle, and he didn't know either.

* Tortoises like George can live for up to **100 years.** And there are tortoises that can live **even longer than that.**

* A giant tortoise named Adwaita lived in Kolkata Zoo in India until he died in 2006, and they think he was born around 1750— so he lived **more than 250 years!** He was born **before** the American Revolution and Abraham Lincoln.

Also Slinky the corn snake.

And a leopard gecko
(which is a type of lizard)

called Jabberwock

after a **monster** in a poem, even though Jabberwock isn't at all like a **monster** and wouldn't hurt a fly. Actually, he **WOULD** totally hurt a fly—**he is a lizard, after all.**

Reptiles aren't easy to look after. They need heating and special living conditions and food. The food is a bit gruesome—things like **crickets and mealworms.** So I'm not allowed to have one, but I visit Alex's pets **a lot.**

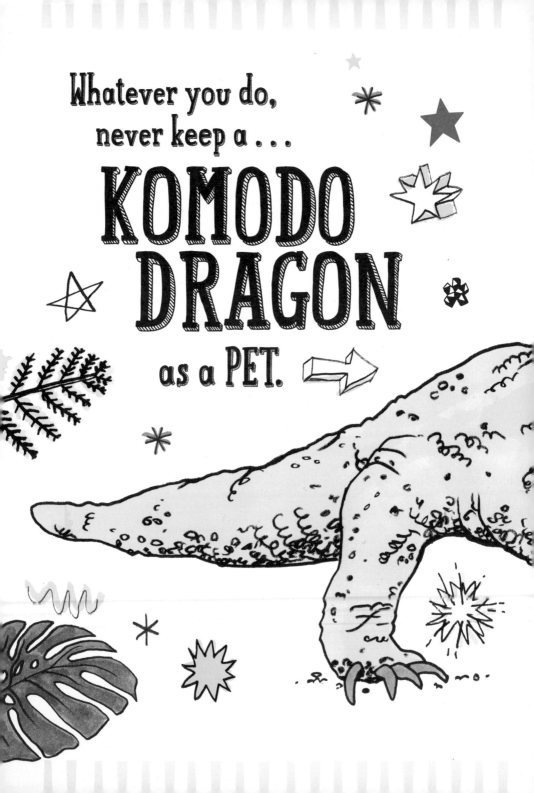

Whatever you do,
never keep a . . .
KOMODO DRAGON
as a PET.

Komodo dragons are

GIANT MEAT-EATING LIZARDS

—the heaviest lizards in the world—found on a few islands in Indonesia. **They are the size and weight of an adult human being,** though the biggest was enormous and weighed **366 pounds (166 kg).**

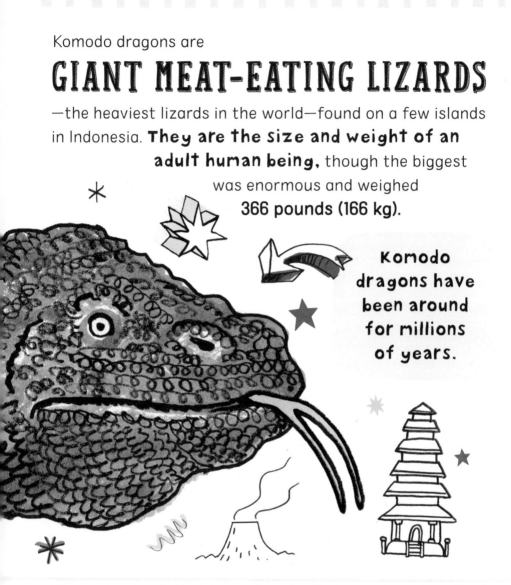

Komodo dragons have been around for millions of years.

They eat animals that have **already died,** and they also attack living animals with their huge **serrated** teeth. If an animal does manage to get away from a Komodo dragon, it will probably die anyway because these **ENORMO-LIZARDS** have a **venomous bite**.

PIGS

DEER

OTHER KOMODO DRAGONS

EVEN PEOPLE

They also have **LOADS of bacteria** in their mouths (they are strangers to dentists). A Komodo dragon will follow and find an animal, even if it can't keep up, because it has a **very good sense of smell**. It uses its long, yellow tongue to sniff things out, like **snakes** do.

* Alex's snake Slinky is a corn snake.

* He is **very friendly** (and NOT venomous) and seems to like slithering around people's arms and necks.

* He eats **defrosted dead mice.**

* Slinky is **20 INCHES (50 CM) LONG.** But the longest snake in the world is **18 TIMES longer than that.**

Reticulated pythons are the
WORLD'S LONGEST SNAKES

* They can measure over **30 feet (9 m) LONG.**

* They're constricting snakes, which means they don't have a **venomous bite** but **squeeze** their prey to death instead.

The longest pet snake is also a reticulated python. She's named **Medusa** and she is:

25 FEET, 2 INCHES (7.67 M) LONG

Sometimes, pet snakes **ESCAPE**. A **royal python** escaped during a house move (if we ever move house I am going to be **REALLY** careful with my pets!) and was found when he came up **out of a toilet**—a big surprise for the five-year-old boy who was about to **go pee**. The snake was about 35 inches (90 cm) long and it wasn't dangerous, but sometimes pet pythons do grow **REALLY** big and **kill their owners!**

So I bet Alex is glad that Slinky will only grow to be about **5 feet (1.5 m) long** at the very most, and won't inject deadly venom or squeeze anybody to death.

Alex and Lily helped me look all over the yard and every last inch of the house (again), except for Mom's bedroom which she said was **Out of Bounds**.

Until **Alex** found some DART GUNS in the back of my wardrobe and that was the end of the search for Twiggy.

To be honest I was more interested in **finding Twiggy** than in shooting Lily and Alex.

I was really glad they came to help though—we looked everywhere.

But they've gone home now and

we still haven't found Twiggy.

It's nearly the end of the weekend. I don't want to go back to school without **finding her**.

Plus it would mean another night for Twiggy **pretending to be a stick** while all sorts of **predators** lurk in the undergrowth.

There's a Swiss cheese plant in the living room so I had a careful look at that, just in case. **There was no stick insect on it,** but it's not an especially twiggy kind of plant so it's not all that surprising.

I'm racking my brains for Twiggy hiding places. But it's getting late and I'm starting to feel like I'll **NEVER** find Twiggy.

I was slumped on the sofa staring at the Swiss cheese plant when **Jess** and **Joe** came to help. Sometimes they are the best brother and sister ever, even though, as Mom says, we **"have different interests."**

THEY ASKED LOTS OF QUESTIONS . . .

Where does **Twiggy** come from?

She came from the **pet shop**, but she's an **Indian stick insect**. They live in **India** and in other places with a **tropical** or **semitropical climate**.

How well do Twiggy and Wiggy get along?

Could Joe mean that **Wiggy** might have EATEN **Twiggy**, or something?

HE HAS A SICK MIND.

They get along **very well**, because they have plenty of space. Stick insects **might** fight one another if they don't have enough space, but **Twiggy** and **Wiggy** have a big **vivarium**.

Have you **REALLY** **checked** the vivarium? Like, **REALLY** carefully?

YES OF COURSE I HAVE! ABOUT 100 TIMES.

Twiggy is a master of disguise.

DON'T FORGET WHAT I SAID ABOUT HIDING IN PLAIN SIGHT.

Joe said.

JESS SAID.

Why don't you check the plants in your room again? Your room has more plants in it than anywhere else. Me and Joe will check the other house plants. Come on!

I knew Twiggy wouldn't be in my bedroom. I must have checked that room

a gazillion times.

But . . . the bramble leaves I'd left on the windowsill looked nibbled.

I started looking at the plants

REALLY CLOSELY.

Nothing on the cactuses . . .

Nothing on the pitcher plant (**thank GOODNESS**) . . .

Nothing on the ferns . . .

HANG ON!

I looked again at the dead leaves on one of the ferns. The ones I was **going to cut off.**

One bit looked as though it was

SWAYING SLIGHTLY...

TWIGGY!

Everyone was **very relieved** that **Twiggy** was back in her vivarium with **Wiggy**.

PHEW!

THANK GOODNESS FOR THAT.

I told you she'd be all right, Sam!

FINALLY!

Mom started vacuuming.

I remembered that I had some homework to do. Luckily, it was about **INVERTEBRATES,** which is one of my **favorite** subjects. (Though I might have been **too sad** to do it if Twiggy was still missing.)

There was a worksheet to do where you have to put animals in the **VERTEBRATES** or **INVERTEBRATES** columns **(easy)** but I added some facts about stick insects and drew Twiggy and Wiggy to make it look more interesting.

Vertebrates (Animals with a backbone)	Invertebrates (Animals without a backbone)
✳ Tortoise	✳ Worm
✳ Corn snake	✳ Jellyfish
✳ Vampire bat	✳ Crab
✳ Shark	✳ Stick insect
✳ Frog	✳ Spider
✳ Komodo dragon	✳ Woodlouse

Twiggy

Wiggy

Some stick insects can make poisonous chemicals ooze out of their legs.

stick insects shed their skin and eat the old one.

Stick insects make GREAT pets.

TURN OVER FOR
EVEN MORE
AMAZING
ANIMAL FACTS

I'm always finding out new facts, and just about **everything is interesting if you think about it enough,** or find out more about it—even, like, concrete. (Actually concrete really is interesting but I'll save that for another time.)

Here are my . . .

TOP TEN
INTERESTING
FACTS ABOUT
ANIMALS

(Although they'll probably have changed by next week as I find out new things.)

1. **Ladybugs** have poisonous knees. If they're attacked, they produce a poisonous yellow stuff from their leg joints that **smells and tastes disgusting** to predators.

2. **Wombats** are the only animal in the world that have **cube-shaped poop.** No one is sure why.

3. You can tell a **blue whale's** age **from its earwax,** because for every year of its life a new layer is added.

4. **Crows** are clever birds. In Japan, they drop nuts on the road for **cars to crack open** as they run over them. Then the birds **wait for the traffic light** to change so they can safely go and eat the nuts.

5. The longest **worm** ever found was a bootlace worm **164 feet (50 m) long.** That's the length of **three and a half buses.**

6. Epaulette sharks can walk on land on their fins. Sometimes the tide goes out and leaves them stranded, but they can waddle between rockpools and get back to the sea.

7. If a predator grabs a **gecko's** tail, the **tail drops off.** But not only that—the tail wriggles and even **SQUEAKS** to make the predator eat that instead of the **rest of the gecko.**

8.  **Dolphins** have names to **identify themselves,** just like we do. Obviously, the names are in dolphin language, which is made up of **whistles and clicks**. Sometimes male dolphins are such good pals that they blend their names together.

9. **Monkeys** peel their bananas **from the bottom,** not the stem end like most people do.

10. Some kinds of **parrot fish** make slime from a special **organ on their heads,** then cover themselves in it to go to sleep, like **revolting slime pajamas.**

AMAZING ANIMALS

and where to find them

Are you desperate to tell someone about fish in slime pajamas, exploding beetles, and what woodlice do instead of peeing? Here's where to find the facts about all of the surprising, disgusting, and incredible animals we've met.